Miraculous Magic Tricks

CLOSE-UP MAGIC

by Mike Lane

Illustrations by David Mostyn

WINDMILL BOOKS

New York

Published in 2012 by Windmill Books, an Imprint of Rosen Publishing
29 East 21st Street, New York, NY 10010

Copyright © 2012 by Arcturus Publishing Ltd.

First Edition

Author: Mike Lane
Editors: Patience Coster and Joe Harris
Illustrations: David Mostyn
Design: Tokiko Morishima

Library of Congress Cataloging-in-Publication Data

Lane, Mike.
 Close-up magic / by Mike Lane.
    p. cm. — (Miraculous magic tricks)
 Includes index.
 ISBN 978-1-61533-515-2 (library binding) —
 ISBN 978-1-4488-6737-0 (pbk.) —
 ISBN 978-1-4488-6738-7 (6-pack)
 1. Magic tricks—Juvenile literature. I. Title.
 GV1548.L34 2012
 793.8—dc23
                          2011028922

Printed in China

For more great fiction and nonfiction, go to www.windmillbooks.com

CPSIA Compliance Information: Batch # AW2102WM: For further information
contact Windmill Books, New York, New York at 1-866-478-0556

SL002052US

CONTENTS

INTRODUCTION

Within these pages you will discover great close-up magic tricks that are easy to do and impressive to watch.

To be a successful magician, you will need to practice the tricks in private before you perform them in front of an audience. An excellent way to practice is in front of a mirror, since you can watch the magic happen before your own eyes.

When performing, you must speak clearly, slowly, and loudly enough for everyone to hear. But never tell the audience what's going to happen.

Remember to "watch your angles." This means being careful about where your spectators are standing or sitting when you are performing. The best place is directly in front of you.

Never tell the secret of how the trick is done. If someone asks, just say: "It's magic!"

THE MAGICIAN'S PLEDGE

I promise not to reveal the secrets of magic to those who are not magicians.

I promise to practice these magic tricks over and over again before attempting to perform them in front of an audience.

I promise to respect my art, the art of magic.

CARD THROUGH TABLE

ILLUSION

A spectator chooses a card from a deck. He returns his card to the deck, which is placed on a table. The magician "slaps" or "taps" the card through the deck and the table.

1 The magician asks a spectator to choose a card from a deck.

2 The magician splits the deck and places the two halves side by side. While doing this, he sneaks a card from the deck and holds it face down in the palm of one hand. He keeps it hidden from the spectator by resting his hand casually on his leg.

MAGICIAN'S TIP!
YOU'LL NEED TO PERFECT THE ART OF "PALMING"—SLIPPING A CARD FROM THE DECK INTO YOUR HAND WITHOUT ANYONE NOTICING. TRY PRACTICING IN FRONT OF A MIRROR UNTIL YOU CAN DO IT QUICKLY AND EASILY.

3 The magician asks the spectator to place his card face down on whichever half of the deck he prefers.

4 Using the hand in which the card is hidden, the magician slaps the pile that contains the spectator's card. While doing this, he places the hidden card on top of it.

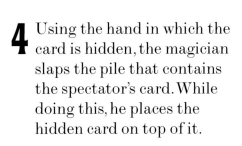

5 The magician taps the deck.

6 He mimes the same action of slapping and tapping with the other deck, but does not place a card on it.

7 The magician now picks up what the spectator believes is his card, but is really the card that the magician had hidden in his hand.

8 The magician places this card on the other deck.

9 The magician picks up the first deck with the spectator's card and places it under the table, directly beneath the deck with the hidden card. The magician asks the spectator to choose whether he wants the magician to slap his card, or tap it.

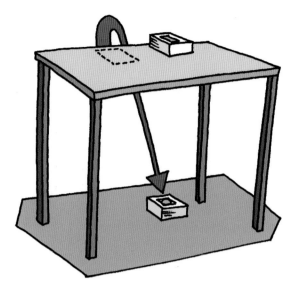

10 The magician does whatever the spectator tells him to do.

11 The magician takes the top card from the deck beneath the table. He shows the spectator his card, which appears to have been "slapped" or "tapped" through the table.

COIN VANISH

ILLUSION

The magician places a coin on a table, covers it with a clear glass tumbler, and the coin vanishes. He removes the tumbler and the coin reappears.

1 Prior to the trick, the magician prepares the tumbler. He places the coin and the tumbler on a piece of red paper.

2 He cuts the paper to fit exactly over the mouth of the tumbler.

3 He glues the paper on to the tumbler.

4 Now he places the tumbler face down on another, larger piece of red paper. The spectator will not be able to see the glued-on piece because it matches the larger piece of paper.

5 To perform the trick, the magician places the coin next to the tumbler.

6 The magician covers the tumbler with a handkerchief. He lifts both tumbler and handkerchief and places them over the coin.

7 The magician removes the handkerchief to show that the coin has vanished. (The coin is now underneath the paper that is glued to the mouth of the tumbler.)

8 The magician covers the tumbler again and lifts the glass and the handkerchief. Hey presto—the coin has reappeared!

THREE-CUP CONFUSION

ILLUSION

The magician places three cups on a table, with one cup the right way up and two cups upside down. He asks the spectator to turn two cups over at the same time. He tells him to do this three times, after which all the cups should be the right way up. The spectator finds this impossible, but the magician can do it easily.

1 The magician places three colored plastic cups so that they are side by side on a table. The middle cup is mouth up, and the two cups on either side are mouth down.

2 The magician explains to the spectator that he must turn over two cups at a time. After the third attempt, all three cups must be mouth up.

13

3 The magician demonstrates this by turning one of the outer cups so that it is mouth up, and the middle cup so that it is mouth down.

4 Next he turns both outer cups so that one is mouth up and the other mouth down.

5 Lastly, he turns both the cups facing mouth down so that they are mouth up. All the cups are now facing mouth up.

6 The magician now turns the middle cup mouth down and tells the spectator to try the trick.

7 The spectator will not be able to do it, because in the original set up the outer cups were mouth down and the middle cup was mouth up.

CRUSHED!

ILLUSION

The magician covers a cup, slides it around on a table, and crushes it, only to reveal that the cup has passed through the table.

1 The magician places a cup mouth down on a table.

2 He covers it with a piece of aluminum foil (no part of the cup should be showing).

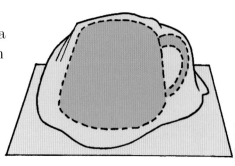

3 The magician moves the foil-covered cup around on the table, forward and backward, side to side, and in a circular motion.

4 The magician continues to do this and then, when he is ready, slides the cup toward him and allows it to fall into his lap without the spectator seeing.

5 The magician allows the foil to retain the shape of the cup and continues sliding it around the table.

6 The magician slides the foil to the middle of the table and crushes it while holding the cup hidden under the table with his other hand.

7 The magician explains that he crushed the cup through the table. He pulls the cup out from under the table to show that it has reappeared in one piece.

SWEEP

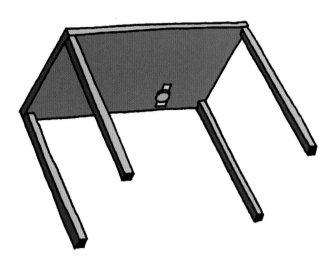

1 Prior to the trick, the magician hides a coin underneath a table. He attaches it to the underside of the table with double-sided tape or wax.

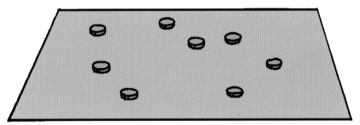

2 To perform the trick, the magician places eight coins on the table and asks a spectator to count them.

3 The magician shows the spectator that his hands are empty and pulls up his sleeves to show he has nothing hidden there either!

4 Positioning himself near the hidden coin, the magician cups one of his hands and begins to sweep the eight coins into it with his other hand.

5 While he is sweeping the coins into his cupped hand, the magician secretly uses this hand to release the hidden coin.

6 He places the coins in the middle of the table again.

7 He asks the spectator to count them. There are now, of course, nine coins.

FRUIT PICKING

ILLUSION

The magician writes down the names of different fruits given by the spectators and places the folded pieces of paper in a bag. When a spectator removes one of the pieces of paper, the magician predicts the fruit written on it.

1 The magician has six pieces of paper, a pen, and a paper bag. He shows the audience that the bag is empty.

2 The magician asks a spectator to name a type of fruit. He writes the name on the first piece of paper, folds it several times, and drops it into the bag. It is important that the spectators do not see what the magician actually writes, so he should have the paper on a pad facing toward himself.

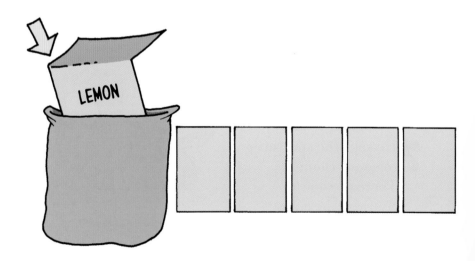

LEMON

3 The magician now asks a second spectator to name a fruit. He pretends to write it down. However, no matter what the spectator says, the magician writes down the name of the first fruit again. The same thing is done with four more spectators. Each time the magician writes down the name of the first fruit, folds the paper, and drops it in the bag.

4 When all six spectators have named their fruit, the magician shakes the bag and asks one of the spectators to reach into the bag and pull out one of the papers.

5 The magician asks the spectator to hold out the folded piece of paper. He slowly waves his hand over the paper and announces the name of the fruit written on it. When the spectator unfolds the paper, they discover that he is correct!

PLATE BALANCE

ILLUSION

The magician balances a plate on a playing card.

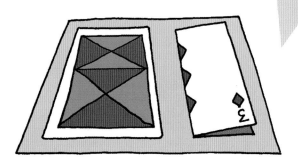

1 Prior to the trick, the magician prepares the playing card by placing it face down on the table. He takes a second card and folds it in half lengthwise so that the face of the card is showing.

GLUE

2 The magician glues the card on the table to one front side of the folded card. The fold should be in the middle. The outside edges of the cards should line up so that they look like one card.

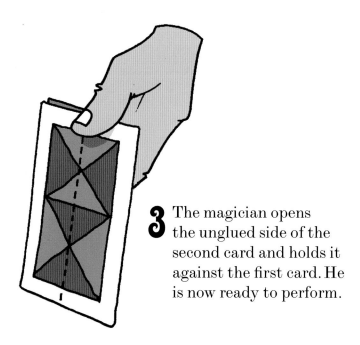

3 The magician opens the unglued side of the second card and holds it against the first card. He is now ready to perform.

4 The magician shows the front and back of the prepared card(s) to the spectator.

5 He places the card on the table in an upright position, holding it with his hand from the side.

6 With his other hand, he places a small plate lightly on the card. Pretending to balance the plate, the magician opens the prepared card to form a T-shape.

7 The magician dramatically removes both his hands. The plate is now balanced on the card.

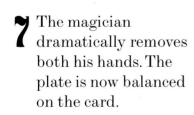

WATER TO ICE

1 Prior to the trick, the magician places a slightly damp bath sponge in the bottom of a cup, making sure it's a snug fit. He puts several ice cubes on top of the sponge.

2 The magician places a bottle of water and an empty clear bowl next to him on the table. He is now ready to perform.

3 He stands in front of the audience and brings out the cup, making sure the inside cannot be seen (the spectators should be seated).

4 The magician picks up the bottle and pours a little water into the cup. (The sponge will absorb the water.)

5 Still being careful not to let the spectators see the inside of the cup, the magician tips it over the bowl and allows the ice cubes to spill out.

IT'S ALIVE!

ABSORBENT COTTON

ILLUSION

The magician picks up a box and removes the lid. Inside is a very pale, real-looking finger that comes to life!

1 Prior to the trick, the magician takes a small cardboard box and lines it with absorbent cotton.

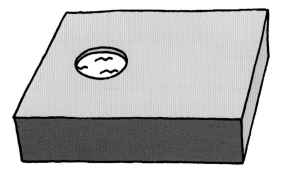

2 The magician cuts a small hole in the bottom of the box. It should just be large enough for him to slip his finger through from underneath. He puts the small box into a larger box.

3 The magician dusts the back of his middle finger with talcum powder. He is now ready to perform.

TALCUM POWDER

4 The magician tells the audience he has a box with a severed finger in it. He reaches into the large box and picks up the small box with both hands.

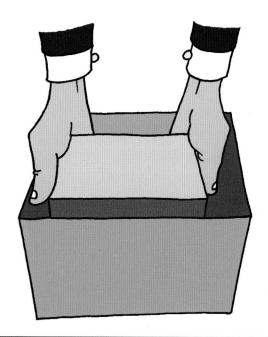

5 As he does so, the magician slips his middle finger through the hole into the box. His finger should be bent so that the back of it covered with powder is showing. The entry hole will be hidden by the absorbent cotton.

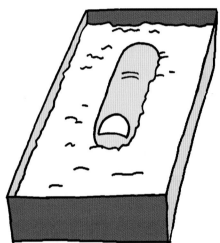

6 The magician now slowly takes the lid off the small box and shows the contents to the audience.

7 While the spectators are looking at the severed finger, the magician tells one of them to touch it. When a spectator does so, the magician moves his finger to show that it is indeed alive!

KNOT

ILLUSION

The magician asks a spectator to try tying a knot in a handkerchief while holding it by two corners. The spectator cannot do this. The magician then shows how it is done.

1 The magician folds his arms so that his right hand is on his left biceps and his left hand grasps his right arm underneath the biceps.

2 The magician takes a corner of a handkerchief with one hand and takes the diagonally opposite corner with the other hand, making sure to keep his arms folded. (This takes practice; it is easier if the spectator hands you the corners.)

3 The magician slowly pulls his hands toward each other. He continues to pull, allowing the handkerchief to form a knot. This is done without letting go of the corners of the handkerchief.

CARD IN POCKET

ILLUSION
The magician has a deck of cards. He removes six cards. One of those cards disappears, and reappears in his pocket.

1 Before he starts the trick, the magician takes a deck of cards and secretly removes one card and places it in his pocket. He makes a mental note of which card it is.

2 In front of the audience, the magician takes six random cards from the deck and places them face down on the table. He hands a spectator a piece of paper and a pen. The magician announces that he will name each card and asks the spectator to write down the name of each card on the paper.

3 The magician turns over the first card and reads out what it is. However, he faces the card toward himself and does not show it to the spectators. He asks the spectator to write down the name of the card and then he slips the card into the deck in a random location.

4 The magician now does the same thing with the other five cards, slipping them into the deck after they have been written down. However, when he gets to the sixth card, the magician does not name the card he is holding. Instead he names the card that is in his pocket.

5 When all the cards have been named, written down, and placed back into the deck, the magician shuffles the deck and hands it to the spectator. He then asks the spectator to find the six cards that were chosen. Of course only five of the cards can be found, because the sixth card named was in the magician's pocket all along.

6 The magician now pulls the missing card from his pocket. It has magically disappeared from the deck and appeared in the magician's pocket.

FURTHER READING

Barnhart, Norm. *Amazing Magic Tricks.* Mankato, MN: Capstone Press, 2008.

Cassidy, John and Michael Stroud. *Klutz Book of Magic.* Palo Alto, CA: Klutz Press, 2006.

Charney, Steve. *Incredible Tricks at the Dinner Table.* Mankato, MN: Capstone Press, 2011.

Klingel, Cynthia. *Magic Tricks.* Mankato, MN: Compass Point Books, 2002.

Tremaine, Jon. *Instant Magic.* Hauppauge, NY: Barron's Educational Series. 2009.

WEB SITES

For Web resources related to the subject of this book, go to: www.windmillbooks.com/weblinks and select this book's title.

GLOSSARY

absorbent (ub-SOR-bent) Able to soak up liquid easily, like a sponge.

double-sided (DUH-bul SY-ded) On both sides.

dramatically (druh-MAT-ik-lee) With drama, in a way that attracts attention.

hey presto (HAY PRES-toh) What magicians say when they mean "suddenly—as if by magic!"

illusion (ih-LOO-shun) An image you can see but is not what it seems to be.

palming (PAH-ming) Hiding something in or with your hand.

INDEX

4/12